Contents

Written by
David Grant

Illustrated by
Nelson Evergreen

Series editor **Dee Reid**

T0346378

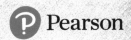 **Pearson**

Before reading *The Girl in the Lake*

New vocabulary

ch1	**p4**	tatty	**ch3**	**p12**	faint
ch1	**p6**	entrance	**ch3**	**p16**	frantically
ch2	**p9**	gazed	**ch4**	**p17**	panted
ch2	**p10**	retrieve	**ch4**	**p19**	insisted

Introduction

Dan, his sister Beth and their parents were driving to Scotland. They were looking for a hotel to spend the night in when Dan saw a tatty old sign which said 'Hill Hall Hotel'. Beside the sign was a little girl in a white dress. She was throwing a red ball into the air and catching it. Beth waved at the girl but the mysterious girl just stared back at her.

The Girl
in the Lake

Chapter One

Dan, his little sister Beth and their parents were driving to Scotland. They had been sitting in the car for hours and they were on the lookout for a hotel for the night.

"Look!" shouted Dan, pointing at a tatty old sign. The paint was peeling off and some of the writing had nearly faded away but they could just make out the words 'Hill Hall Hotel'.

"Great!" said Dad. "That's where we'll stay tonight."

A little girl in a white dress was standing
by the hotel sign. She was throwing a red
ball into the air and catching it. As the car went
by, Beth smiled and waved at her. The young girl
just stared at them with her bright green eyes. She
didn't smile or wave back.

As they walked up to the hotel entrance, Beth

cried, "There she is again!"

The little girl in the white dress was standing by

a big lake in the gardens. She was tossing her ball

into the air and catching it. Beth waved at the girl

but the girl didn't wave back.

"Please can I go and play with her?" asked Beth.

"Maybe later," said Mum.

The hotel smelled dusty and damp. The lights were dim and the carpet was almost worn out.

An elderly woman came to meet them. Her hair was grey and her skin was deathly pale.

"Good evening," she said. "Welcome to Hill Hall Hotel."

But Dan didn't feel very welcome. He felt cold and he had a strange feeling about the hotel.

Chapter Two

The old lady showed them to their room which was large and gloomy.

"Is the little girl in the white dress staying at the hotel?" asked Beth.

The old lady smiled showing her yellow teeth.

"You are the only guests," she said.

"Does the little girl live nearby?" asked Dad.

"There are no other houses for miles," she replied.

"Who is she then?" asked Beth.

The old lady gazed at Beth. Then she said,

"Many years ago, a little girl named Lucy lived

at Hill Hall. One day, Lucy was playing in

the gardens with her favourite toy – a red ball –

when, suddenly, her ball bounced into the lake."

"Lucy reached into the lake to retrieve her ball," continued the old lady, "but she lost her balance and fell in. She drowned before anyone could rescue her. And her ghost has wandered the hotel grounds ever since."

Beth went white and grabbed her mum's hand.

"It's just a silly story," said Dad, putting his arm around Beth.

"Believe me, it's a true story," said the old lady. Then she gave a strange smile.

Dan began to wish he had never seen the tatty old hotel sign.

Chapter Three

The next morning, Mum and Dad were packing up.

"Can we go outside and play?" begged Beth.

"OK, but be careful," warned Mum.

"Look after your sister," Dad called to Dan as the children ran out into the bright sunshine.

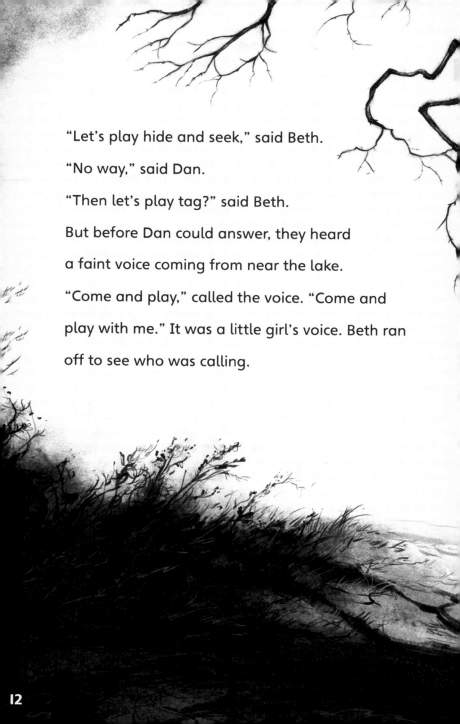

"Let's play hide and seek," said Beth.

"No way," said Dan.

"Then let's play tag?" said Beth.

But before Dan could answer, they heard

a faint voice coming from near the lake.

"Come and play," called the voice. "Come and

play with me." It was a little girl's voice. Beth ran

off to see who was calling.

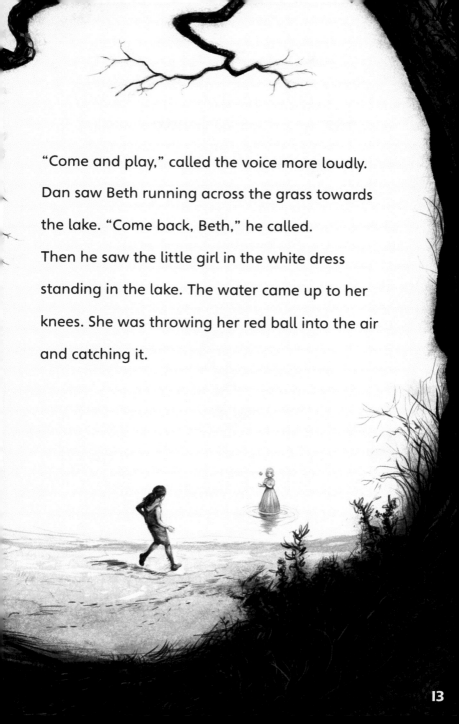

"Come and play," called the voice more loudly.
Dan saw Beth running across the grass towards
the lake. "Come back, Beth," he called.

Then he saw the little girl in the white dress
standing in the lake. The water came up to her
knees. She was throwing her red ball into the air
and catching it.

"Come and play," called the little girl again.

Beth stepped into the lake. The water came up to her knees.

"Beth!" shouted Dan as he started running towards the lake.

He saw the little girl grab hold of Beth's arm and pull her deeper into the lake. The water was now up to their waists.

"Beth, stop!" yelled Dan.

But the little girl was dragging Beth further and further into the lake. The water came up to their necks. The little girl turned round and smiled at Dan, her green eyes burning brightly.

Then he watched in horror as Beth and the little girl disappeared beneath the water.

"No!" shouted Dan, as he charged into the lake.

The water was freezing but Dan didn't notice.
He looked around wildly for Beth. Then he dived
under the water but it was too cloudy and murky
to see.

As he searched frantically, Dan remembered what
his dad had said. *"Look after your sister."*
He felt sick. "Beth!" he screamed. "Beth!"

Chapter Four

Dan sprinted back to the hotel as fast as he could. His mum and dad were in the lounge drinking coffee.

"What on earth have you been doing?" said his mum. "You're soaking wet!"

"Beth went in the lake," panted Dan. "I tried to find her but…"

Then he noticed Beth sitting on the floor. She was drawing a picture. It was a picture of a little girl in a white dress.

"How did you get back here so quickly?" demanded Dan.

Slowly, Beth turned and looked at him.

"You're not even wet!" said Dan, amazed.

"What are you talking about, Dan?" asked Mum.

"More coffee?" asked the old lady. They all jumped. They hadn't seen her come in.

"I saw the girl in the white dress pull Beth into the lake," insisted Dan.

"What girl?" asked Beth. She sounded surprised. Then the old lady gave a strange smile.

As Dad drove away from the hotel, Beth pulled something out of her pocket. Dan turned to look. He froze. It was a red ball. Beth threw it into the air and caught it. She turned to face Dan. Her dark brown eyes turned green and burnt brightly. "Come and play," she said, throwing the ball to him – and she smiled.

Quiz

Literal comprehension
p7 What evidence is there that the hotel is old?
p10 What had happened to Lucy?
p18 Why is Dan surprised when he gets back to the hotel?

Inferential comprehension
p10 Why does Dad put his arm around Beth?
p14 Why does Beth step into the lake?
p19 Why does Beth say "What girl?"

Personal response
- Would you want to spend the night in Hill Hall Hotel?
- Who do you think the little girl is?
- What do you think has happened to Beth?

Author's style

p7 How does the author make the old lady seem scary?
p16 How does the author convey Dan's panic?
p20 What words does the author use to show that Dan is shocked to see the red ball?

Characters

- **Old Lady** (the hotel owner)
- **Beth** (a girl, aged 10)
- **Dad**
- **Dan** (Beth's brother, aged 13)

Setting the scene

Beth, Dan and their parents are on their way to Scotland but they have stopped for the night at a hotel called Hill Hall Hotel. The hotel is old and dusty and the floor creaks. Beth and Dan think it's really creepy and the old lady who owns the hotel is creepy too.

Old Lady: *(opening a bedroom door)* Here we are. This is your room.

Beth: Look at the gross cobwebs!

Dad: Ssssh! Beth!

Beth: And the floor creaks.

Dan: Dad, tell her to shut up.

Beth: And it smells funny.

Dad: Beth! Don't be so rude.

Old Lady: I'm sorry if the floor creaks but it's an old house.

Beth: This place is really creepy.

Dan: You're creepy.

Dad: Stop it you two!

Beth: Is that little girl we saw by the hotel sign staying at the hotel?

Old Lady: You are the only guests in the hotel tonight.

Dad: Does the little girl live nearby?

Old Lady: There are no other houses for miles around.

Dan: If she isn't staying here and she doesn't live nearby, who is she?

Old Lady: Her name is Lucy.

Beth: Can I play with her?

Old Lady: Of course you can.

Dad: But who is the little girl?

Old Lady: Long ago Hill Hall was not a hotel. Lucy lived here with her family...

Dan: But that doesn't make sense. If she was a little girl many years ago, she'd be grown up by now.

Old Lady: But Lucy never grew up. You see, one day she was playing in the gardens with her favourite toy – a little red ball.

Beth: The girl I saw outside was playing with a little red ball!

Old Lady: *(smiling)* It's the same girl.

Dan: What happened to her?

Old Lady: Lucy's ball bounced into the lake. She ran to the lake to get it. But she slipped and fell in.

Beth: Was she OK?

Old Lady: No, she was not. You see, Lucy couldn't swim.

Dan: Didn't someone see her?

Old Lady: Her parents saw it happen.

Beth: Why didn't they save her?

Old Lady: They tried to save her. But they were too late. By the time they pulled her out of the lake she was dead.

Dad: What a terrible story!

Dan: But that doesn't make sense. We just saw her by the hotel sign, how can she be dead?

Old Lady: She died many years ago. And ever since then her ghost has wandered the grounds of Hill Hall Hotel.

Beth: So the girl that we saw playing with the little red ball is a ghost?

Dad: Of course she isn't a ghost.

Old Lady: Don't you think so?

Dad: No!

Dan: I don't believe in ghosts.

Dad: You're right. There are no such things as ghosts. It's just a silly story.

Old Lady: Really? Then perhaps you can explain something to me.

Dan: Explain what?

Old Lady: The things that my guests tell me.

Dan: What sort of things?

Old Lady: That they have seen a little girl in the gardens playing with a red ball. Or heard a little girl calling them to come and play with her.

Beth: I saw her. We all saw her. We saw a ghost!

Old Lady: I hope you enjoy your stay at Hill Hall Hotel.

Quiz

Text comprehension

p24, 25 & 27 How can you tell Dan is not convinced by the tale of the little girl?

p29 Who believes the old lady's story?

p29 What is the effect of the old lady saying she hopes they enjoy their stay at the hotel?

Vocabulary

p23 Find a word meaning 'makes a squeaky noise'.

p27 Find a word meaning 'walked around'.

p28 Find a word meaning 'make clear'.

Before reading Scared for Fun

Find out about

• the kind of things that scare people.

New vocabulary

p35 phantom
p35 opera
p37 macabre

p37 certificate
p38 paranormal

Introduction

Lots of people like to be scared, so they read scary stories or watch horror films. Some early films scared people even though they were not horror films. When audiences first saw a film of a train heading straight for the camera they thought it was going to come through the screen and squash them!

Scared for Fun

Lots of people like to read scary stories.
Some of the first stories ever told were
ghost stories. Today people still like to
read stories about scary creatures and
they also like to watch scary films.

In 1895, a film was made called 'Train Pulling into a Station'. It was not a horror film. It just showed a train heading towards the camera.

But people in the audience thought the train was really going to squash them! They were so scared that they ran out of the cinema!

The very first scary film was made in 1896. It was called 'The Haunted Castle' and it was just three minutes long. It was a silent film in black and white. In the film, a bat flies into a castle and turns into a devil. Two men in the castle are scared by a skeleton and some ghostly creatures wearing bed sheets. You might not think it sounds very scary, but cinema audiences had not seen scary things on film before and they were really scared.

Lon Chaney as The Phantom of the Opera in 1925

One of the first horror feature films was made in 1925. It was called 'The Phantom of the Opera' and it was about a phantom who haunted an opera house. The film starred Lon Chaney. Lon Chaney did all his own horror make-up to make the Phantom look really scary. He even had a plaster model made of his head to practise his make-up on. When the film was first shown, the audience were so scared that some people fainted.

Bela Lugosi as Dracula in 1931

The first Dracula film was made in the 1920s. Since then there have been more than 160 films about Dracula. The 1931 film, 'Dracula', was very successful so the studios started making lots more horror films like 'Frankenstein', 'The Mummy' and 'The Wolf Man'. The adverts for these films said they were so scary that some of the audience fainted. This might not have been true but it made everyone want to go and see the films!

In the 1950s, a film was made called 'Macabre'. The film-makers said it was so scary they had nurses in the cinema to help people if they fainted. They even had ambulances outside the cinema. Everyone who bought a ticket was given a certificate by the film-makers. The certificate promised to pay their family $1000 if they died of fright as they watched the film. The nurses, the ambulances and the certificates were all fakes, but it made lots of people go and see the film.

Film-makers still use lots of tricks to make people pay to be scared. Most film trailers show clips from the film. But when 'Paranormal Activity' came out in 2009, the trailer didn't show clips of the film – it showed clips of an audience watching the film. It showed the audience covering their eyes and screaming.

The advert worked – 'Paranormal Activity' is one of the most successful films ever made. It cost just $15,000 to make and made $200 million. That is a scary amount of money, all paid by people who like to be scared for fun!

Quiz

Text comprehension

Literal comprehension
p33 Why were audiences scared by the film
'Train Pulling into a Station'?
p35 How did Lon Chaney make the film more scary?
p37 What clever publicity stunt did the makers of
'Macabre' use?

Inferential comprehension
p31 How can you tell people like to read scary stories?
p34 Why might modern audiences not find
'The Haunted Castle' scary?
p38 Why do film-makers use tricks in their trailers?

Personal response
• Do you like scary stories or films?
• Have you ever been too scared to sleep after
watching a film?
• Why do you think people like to be scared?

Non-fiction features

p34 Think of a heading for this page.
p37 How could you divide the information about
'Macabre' into three bullet points?
p38 What punctuation is used instead of the word
'because' in the second paragraph?

Published by Pearson Education Limited, Edinburgh Gate, Harlow, Essex, CM20 2JE.

www.pearsonschoolsandfecolleges.co.uk

Text © Pearson Education Limited 2012

Edited by Bethan Phillips
Designed by Tony Richardson and Siu Hang Wong
Original illustrations © Pearson Education Limited 2012
Illustrated by Nelson Evergreen
Cover design by Siu Hang Wong
Picture research by Melissa Allison
Cover illustration © Pearson Education Limited 2012

The right of David Grant to be identified as author of this work has been asserted by him in
accordance with the Copyright, Designs and Patents Act 1988.

First published 2012

16
24

British Library Cataloguing in Publication Data
A catalogue record for this book is available from the British Library

ISBN 978 0 435 07153 0

Printed and bound in Great Britain by Bell and Bain Ltd, Glasgow

Acknowledgements
The author and publisher would like to thank the following individuals and organisations for
permission to reproduce photographs:

(Key: b-bottom; c-centre; l-left; r-right; t-top)

Ronald Grant Archive: 32-33, Universal Pictures 36; Getty Images: Moviepix 1, 35; Masterfile
UK Ltd: Graham French 38; Rex Features: Everett Collection 37; Shutterstock.com: Dmitrijs
Bindemanis 31, donatas1205 32-33c, Michaela Stejskalova 34

Cover images: Back: Shutterstock.com: Michaela Stejskalova

All other images © Pearson Education

Every effort has been made to contact copyright holders of material reproduced in this book. Any
omissions will be rectified in subsequent printings if notice is given to the publishers.